Working Together in the Classroom

CIVIC VIRTUES

Simone Braxton

I0807537

CIVICS FOR THE REAL WORLD™

Rosen Classroom™

You can use teamwork at school. You work with your classmates all the time.

Your teacher might put you in a group. Some groups are small. Some groups are big.

Each person in a group has special skills. Use your skills to help others learn.

Do you know how to use a tablet? You could teach your classmates.

Science projects are often done in groups. Remember to share the microscope!

You can get more done when you work together. Everyone has a job to do.

You might not like everyone in your group. Be nice and try to get along.

You can share a map or a globe. Sharing is a great way to make friends.

Teamwork helps things get done faster. It can also help things get done better.

It's good to work together in the classroom. It makes learning more fun!

WORDS TO KNOW

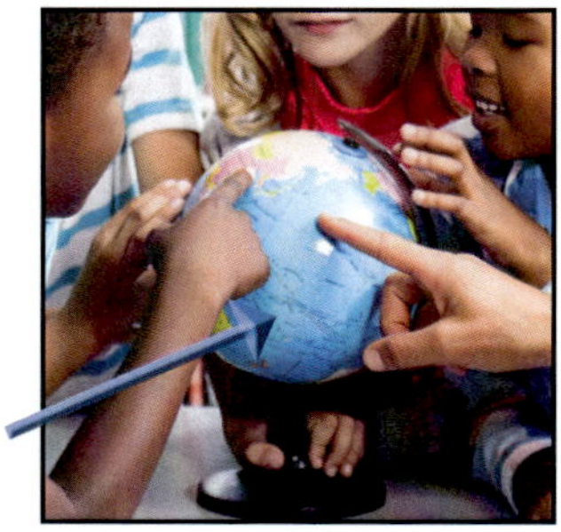

globe

microscope

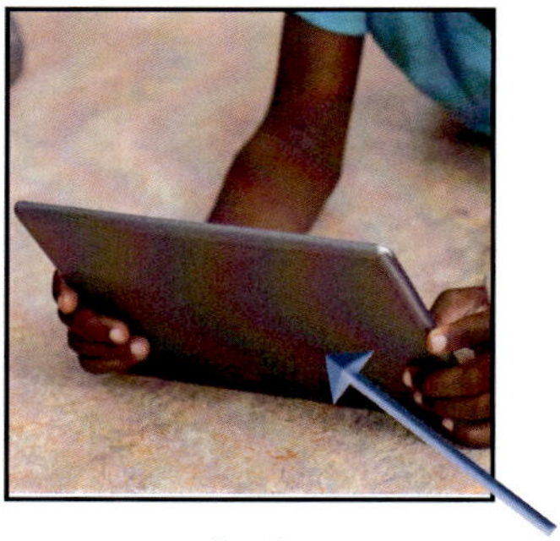

tablet